Manufactured in Altona, Manitoba, Canada in
February 2012 by Friesen

First Edition

16 15 14 13 12   15 14 13 12 11 10 9 8 7 6 5 4 3 2

Published by
Gibbs Smith
P.O. Box 667
Layton, Utah 84041

1.800.835.4993 orders
www.gibbs-smith.com

Designed by Renee Bond

Gibbs Smith books are printed on either
recycled, 100% post-consumer waste, FSC-
certified papers or on paper produced from
sustainable PEFC-certified forest/controlled
wood source. Learn more at www.pefc.org.

ISBN: 978-1-4236-2483-7

Draw yourself as a superhero.

Draw an evil robot attacking the city.

Create a hero super enough
to save the city.

Draw a cape for PEACOCK GIRL.

Draw awesome wings on
the MASKED EAGLE.

Give these superheroes
heroic faces.

Give these supervillains evil hair.

Draw a superhuman that can walk up the side of a building.

Create a hero that has the power of a magnet.

Draw the EVIL ERASER.

Draw a real superhero: a police officer from your town.

CAUTION-POLICE LINE-

-DO NOT CROSS-

Draw a firefighter in action.

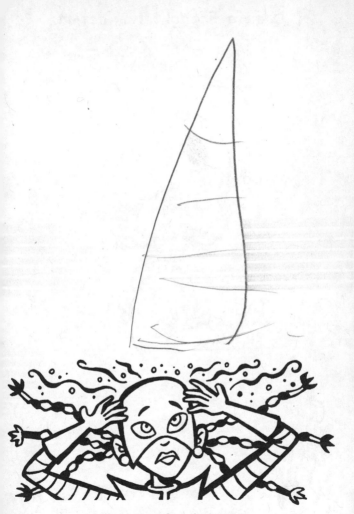

What is the heroine
lifting with her mind?

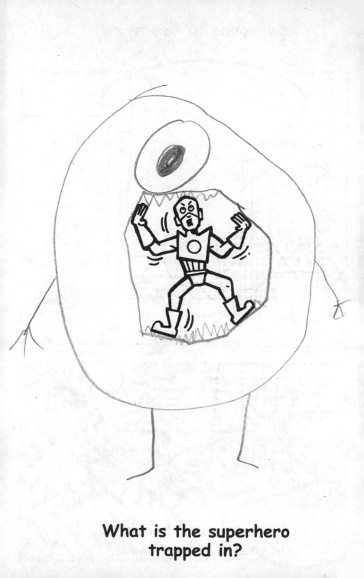

What is the superhero trapped in?

Add words to this story.

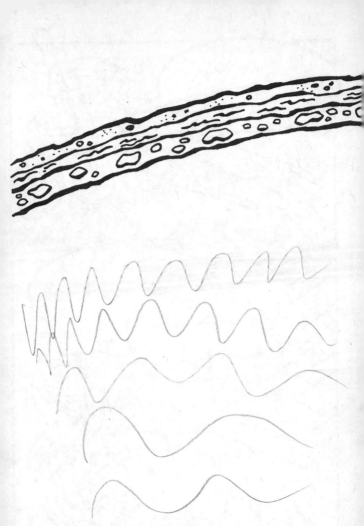

What does the hero find in the center of the Earth?

flames

Draw a hero that can out-fly a missile.

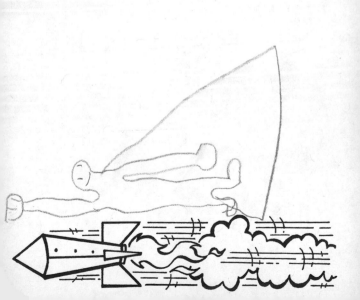

What superhero will stop this meteor?

shield
man

Draw the super students
flying to Superhero School.

Draw the leader of this superhero team.

Draw the leader of this supervillain group.

Draw the superhuman lifting this old car.

Create a hero that can stop this train.

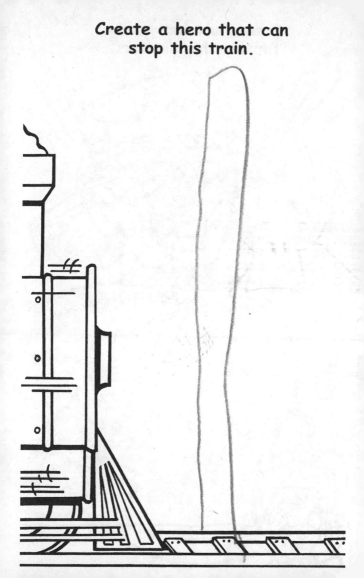

Draw the hero's hotline.

Draw PEANUT BUTTER MAN's sidekick called the JELLY KID.

Draw a superhero changing in the phone booth.

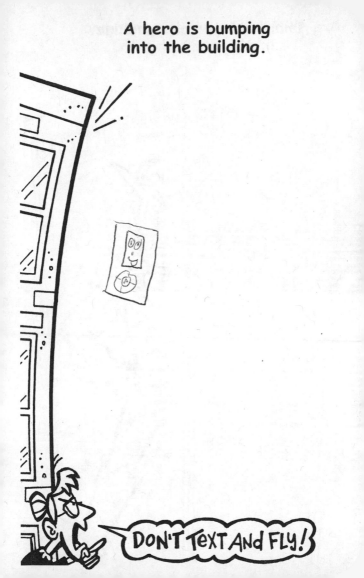

This hero is half machine.

Draw SKUNK MAN's
super stinky tail.

Draw the hero being hit
by the freeze ray.

Design a superhero's shield.

The crowd fears the supervillain.

The crowd cheers the arrival of the superhero!

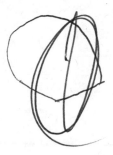

Design MUSCLE MAN's awesome super muscle car.

Draw MIGHTY MOM's flying super minivan.

Draw two superstrong heroes in a tug of war.

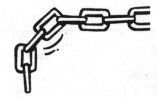

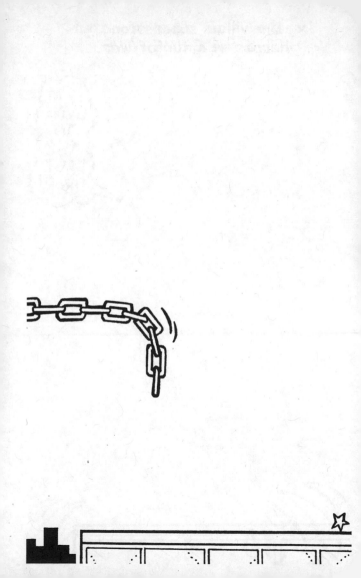

Draw a villain made of water called the CRIME WAVE.

Create a superhero made of a sponge.

Draw your parents (or two special people in your life) as high-flying superheroes.

What's on the racks in the Superhero Store?

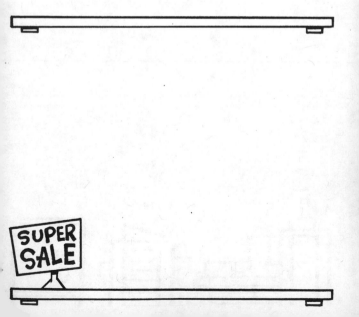

SUPER
SALE

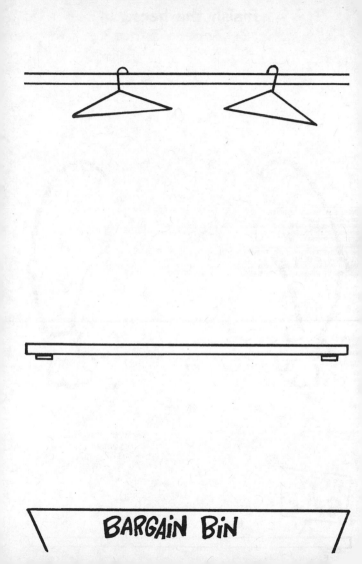

BARGAIN BIN

Finish the hero.

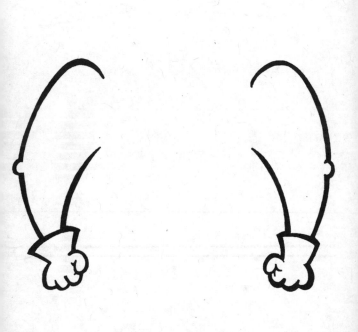

Draw the rest of the heroine.

Draw all the tattoos on the *TATTOO TITAN*.

Create a superhero that controls electricity.

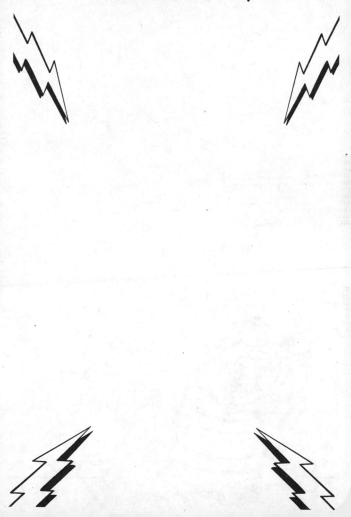

Create a hero that can defeat this giant worm.

Draw a superhero that can stop the invading alien.

Draw a giant superhero that towers over the city.

Create a tiny superhero climbing this pencil point.

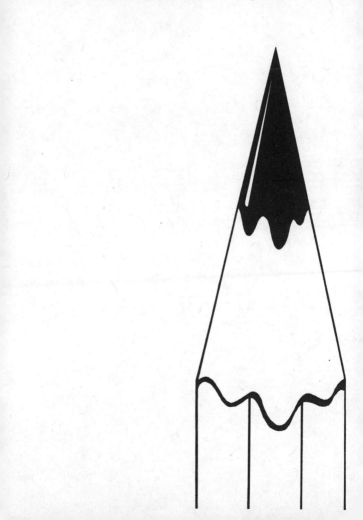

Create BAD BUTTERFLY,
a beautiful villain.

Draw the heroic SUPER STINK BUG.

Draw the inside of your brain where the BLOOD CELL DEFENDER fights crime.

The BLOOD CELL DEFENDER
battles the VIRUS VILLAIN.

It's the SUPER SNEEZER.

COOTIE GIRL spreads disgusting
cooties all over the school.

10-9-8-7-6-5-4-3-2-1!
Draw BLASTOFF BOY.

Create the AMAZING ARCHER
on his flying arrow.

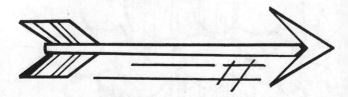

Draw the supervillain's evil giant brain.

The *FISHY FOE* has huge lobster claws.

HOW CAN I DOODLE MY WAY OUT OF THIS?

Draw the rest of the clay monster
that has CAPTAIN DOODLE.

Draw CAPTAIN DOODLE's sword
fight with the PAINTING PIRATE.

Draw the superhero
this kid turns into.

Draw what this hero eats
that gives him superpowers.

Draw a supervillain toy.

Create a hero for the toy box.

Create bodies for these supervillains.

Draw this hero's super expressions.

SURPRISE

FEAR

ANGER

PAIN

LAUGHiNG

THOUGHTFUL

TiRED

HAPPY

MIND READER GIRL is reading your mind right now. Draw what she sees.

This hero with X-ray vision sees someone heroic in your school. Draw who he sees.

Who is this strong?

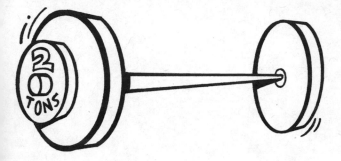

Who can fly this high?

Change this average family into a family of superheroes.

Draw the smartest person you know as the BRAIN WONDER.

Draw the funniest person you know as the LAUGH MASTER.

THE ONLY PUNCHES I THROW ARE PUNCHLINES!

Create the red-hot
hero BOILING BOY.

**Draw his classmate, the
super-cold GOOSEBUMP GIRL.**

Draw your teacher
as a superhero.

Turn his piece of chalk into an evil CHALK MONSTER.

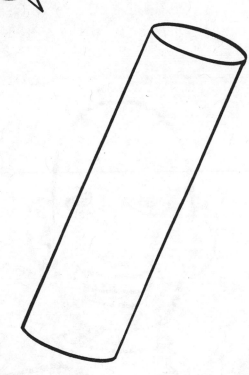

Draw a mask and headgear
for the *HELICOPTER HERO*,
guardian of the skies.

Create a costume for MALL
GIRL, guardian of the mall.

Draw the SKY QUEEN, who can control the weather.

The sinister **SMOG HOG** is **SKY QUEEN**'s enemy.

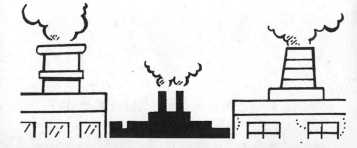

Who's grabbing this hero's cape?

Draw what superheroes
do on their day off.

Draw a prehistoric superhero.

Create a hero of the future.

Give Uncle Sam a superhero body.

Draw the Statue of Liberty
as a super heroine.

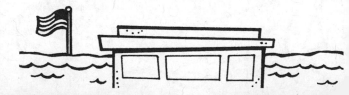

What do heroes get for their birthdays?

What do superhumans eat for breakfast?

This rock 'n' roll superhero travels on a giant flying guitar.

Create a sidekick for the rocker hero.

Draw SUPER SPAGHETTI MAN and his mighty meatball weapon.

Draw the pointy PORCUPINE GUY.

Draw this bad guy's laser ray gun weapon.

Create KNIGHT GUY's super sword.

Create MASSIVE MAN, a
very heavy superhero.

Draw UN-GRAVITY GIRL, a very light crime fighter.

The CRAFTY CREEP is shooting CAPTAIN DOODLE with a glue gun.

CAPTAIN DOODLE battles the EVIL PAPER DOLL.

Who's fighting the creature?

What hero hitched a ride on this airplane?

Draw PRETZEL MAN's
twisted body.

Draw the melted half
of MS. MELTDOWN.

Draw a TV superhero.

Draw the hero flying off the 3D movie screen.

Draw FLEX MAN's stretched-out arms.

HERE COMES THE LONG ARM OF THE LAW!

Design FLEX MAN's flying patrol car.

Create the art for this comic.

What's sneaking up on the hero?

What does the heroine see on the danger screen?

Who's fighting the shark?

Who's stopping this fire creature?

Design the inside of the CAT CRUSADER's secret hero headquarters.

SUPER LiTTER BOX

Draw the lunch room
TRASH MONSTER.

Only SUPER CUSTODIAN MAN
can stop trash monster.

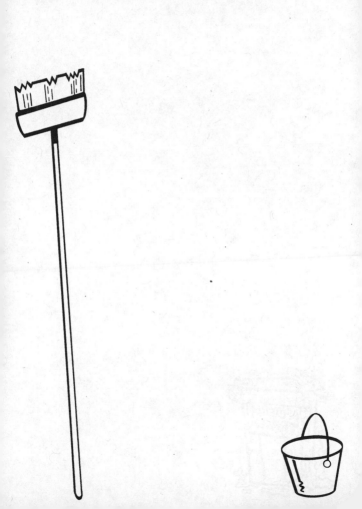

How would you draw an invisible hero?

Draw the hero breaking through the brick wall.

Create bodies for these
circus superheroes.

Create the SUPER DUPER SNOWBOARDER.

Draw the rest of the SNOWBOARDER's foe, the SINISTER SNOWMAN.

Create the controller of all bubbles, the BUBBLE MASTER.

Turn this rubber ducky
into a superhero.

Draw the other half of
this hero's face.

Draw the other half of
this heroine's face.

Create a magician that fights crime.

Make his rabbit sidekick appear.

The super strong SANDSTONE
is a hero made of sand.

Design SANDSTONE's sand castle headquarters.

CAPTAIN DOODLE battles a
creepy CRAYON CREATURE.

CAPTAIN DOODLE meets the DOODLE DIVA.

Draw all the superpowered kids at Super Tot Daycare.

RULES:
NO
FLYING!
NO
INVISIBILITY!
NO
FLAMES!

HOW DO YOU
BABYSIT
SUPERKIDS!

Draw a sports athlete who is a hero to you.

Create the HOCKEY HERO.

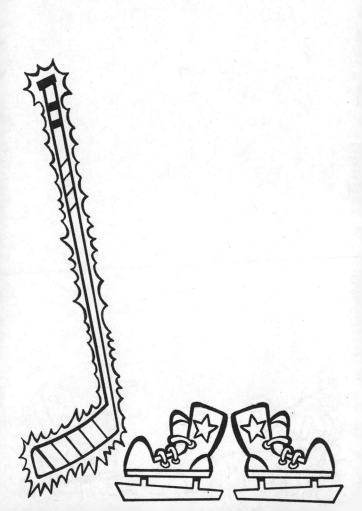

Create the hero of the night,
the mysterious DARK OWL.

Draw the villain melting a hole in this vault.

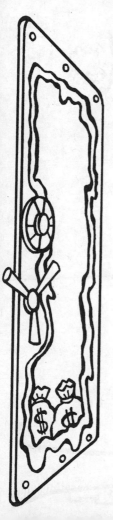

What do superheroes wear for pajamas?

Draw this supervillain's teddy bear.

Who saved Humpty Dumpty?

Draw COW MAN jumping over the moon.

He's HALF MAN, HALF COW, BUT ALL HERO!

Create a superhero that
fights crime in space.

Draw the space hero's
super spaceship.

TARANTULA GIRL has eight arms. Draw them.

Draw the many legs of the CATERPILLAR KID.

The FRENCH FRY FIEND has captured the salt shaker.

BURGER BOY to the rescue.

Draw MIGHTY MOTHER NATURE, guardian of the Earth.

Create the FANTASTIC FATHER TIME, the TICK TOCK TITAN.

**Who's hanging out on
Superhero Street?**

Who's hiding out in Villain Valley?

Create the GUARDIAN OF THE JUNGLE.

Draw the *JUNGLE HERO's* wild animal sidekick.

The carpet-riding villain is stealing the prince's lamp.

Draw the superhero genie bursting from the lamp.

**Show what you would make a
superhero do by remote control.**

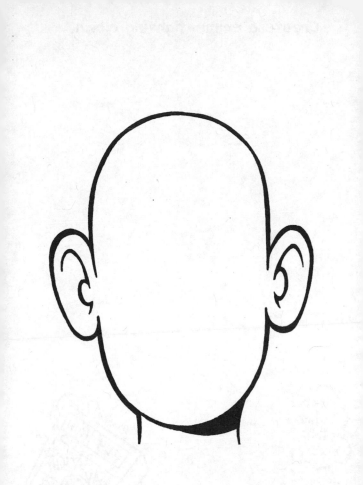

Draw your expression if you were
to meet your favorite superhero.

Create a crime-fighting clown.

HE'S SUPER AND SILLY!

HE'S A HA HA HERO!

Draw the crime-fighting clown's funny little supercar.

Who is fast enough to capture the ROLLING RASCAL?

Create WONDER WHEELMAN's superhero wheelchair.

The *TREE KING* has branches
for arms and legs.

The PLANT PRINCESS wears
a costume of leaves.

Change this bowling pin into an evil supervillain.

THIS PIN WILL STRIKE BACK!

Create the hero named the SUPER BOWLER.

Finish the comic book cover.

Finish the wanted poster.

Create bodies for these holiday heroes.

Draw the hero she
suddenly changes into.

Create the supervillain the
mad scientist becomes.

Finish drawing the hero known as the BULLDOG.

Turn the BULLDOG's dog house into a superhero headquarters.

The evil CAPTAIN COCKROACH
leads the BAND OF BAD BUGS.

Create the SUPER PARK PROTECTOR.

Create the bodies for these superhero house pets.

Create the superhuman named MATH MAN.

Draw the hero called the SUPER SPELLER.

Draw the bottom half
of SNAKE KID.

Draw the top half of
GIRAFFE GIRL.

Draw a new superhero
bumping into everything,
learning how to fly.

Draw the upside-down hero
called UPSIDE-DOWN MAN.

VOLCANO KID's head is erupting.

LADY SPARKLER leaves a cool trail of fireworks.

Draw BOOMERANG BOY.

Draw the SUPER SCREAMER.

This girl is a super heroine
in her dreams.

This boy is a supervillain
in his nightmares.

The mini hero, MS. MICRO,
battles an evil fly.

MS. MICRO attacks the DECAY DEVIL in your mouth.

Make this guy into a superhero.

Create a hero made of
sandwiches called the
HERO SANDWICH.

Draw SOUPER MAN.

Draw the guests at this superhero party.

PLEASE HANG UP YOUR CAPE!

Draw a hero that fights crime on this surfboard.

Create a hero that travels on a super skateboard.

Draw a super battle that goes with these sound effects.

It's the youngest superhero, the *TODDLER TITAN!*

Oh no! It's *TODDLER TITAN*'s
stinkiest foe, the *LIVING DIAPER*.

Draw the power rays the heroes
are shooting at the giant foe.

Draw the giant foe the
heroes are shooting at.

Finish drawing the hero called FLYING PIG BOY.

Create the talkative hero named SUPER CHATTERER.

Create the portraits in the Superhero Museum.

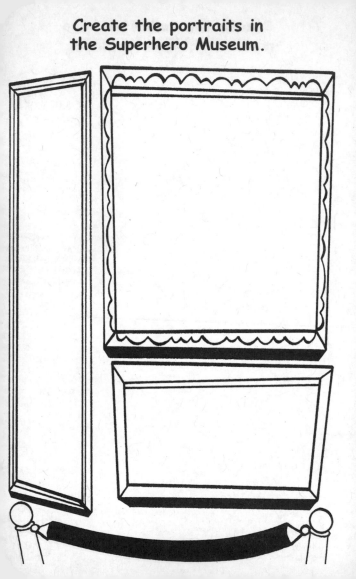

Draw the villain who is stealing the masterpieces.

The SINISTER SCULPTOR is attacking CAPTAIN DOODLE.

It's the GUARDIAN OF
THE PLAYGROUND.

Draw the HULA HOOP HERO.

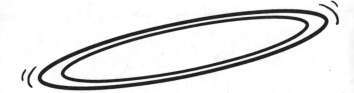

A superhero is patrolling
near your home. Draw
your neighborhood.

Draw the protector of cyberspace, the COMPUTER KID.

Draw the heroes in this high-flying superhero race.

Draw the hero that Larry
the Librarian changes into.

Draw the POWER PROFESSOR's secret identity.

The high-flying BIRD WOMAN is marrying the MIGHTY MERMAN at this superhero wedding.

Years later, BIRD WOMAN and the MIGHTY MERMAN have a child with both their powers.

Turn these historical people into superheroes.

BEN FRANKLIN

SHAKESPEARE

A PiLGRiM

ELViS

Create their greatest foes.

The ELECTRIC ZAPPER

STAGE FRiGHT

The JERKY TURKEY

The TUNELESS TERROR

Draw the left side of superfast BROTHER BLUR.

Draw the right side
of SISTER SQUID.

This hero can't fly and
has to take the bus.

Your toilet is secretly
a crime fighter.

Create a ghost-busting superhero named HAUNT HUNTER.

Draw a ghost supervillain.

Draw this villainess's expressions.

THINKING ABOUT A CRIME

EVIL LAUGHTER

STUNNED BY A HERO

SADNESS IN PRISON

This superhuman is half hero and half villain. Draw his villain half.

Draw the weapons in the Supervillain Evil Weapon Warehouse.

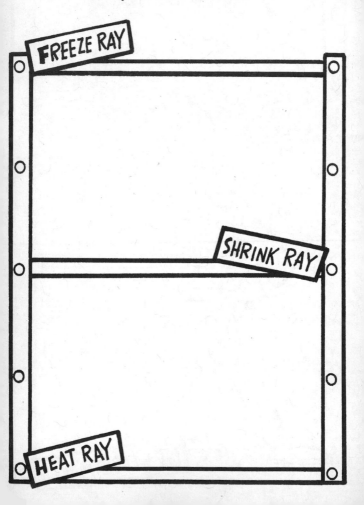

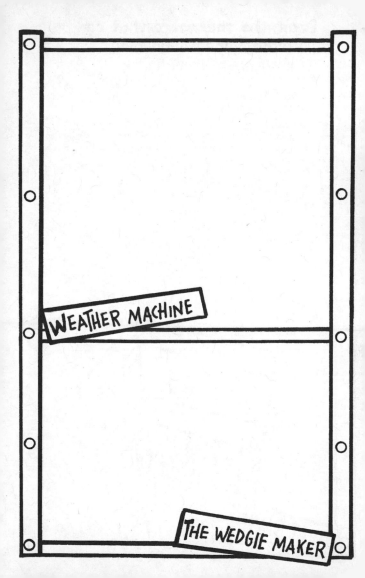

Draw the superhero that can leap over this building.

Create the hero swinging across the night sky.

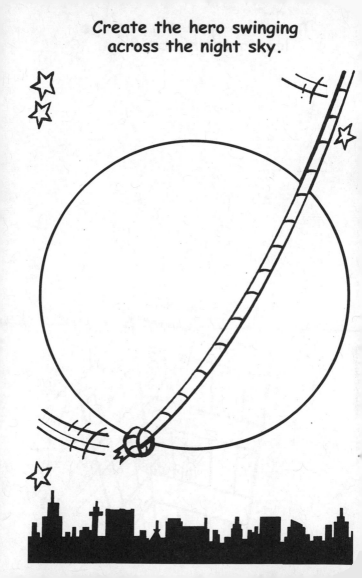

Draw the hero stopping the bad guy's submarine.

Who can defeat the GIANT GINGERBREAD MAN?

Draw your own family as
a superhero team.

Create a sidekick for
CAPTAIN DOODLE.

Can you draw CAPTAIN DOODLE?

Create your own superhero comic.

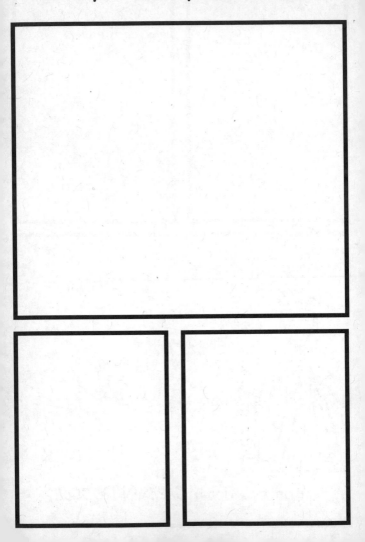

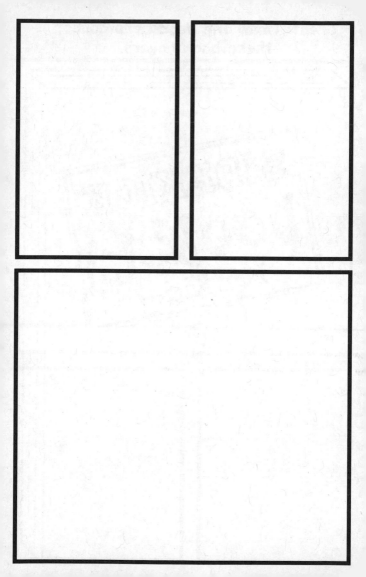

Draw the doodles on
these book covers.

Find and finish these heroes, which appear somewhere in this book.

Draw a big super battle
between the heroes and villains
you've created in this book.

What are all these heroes fighting?

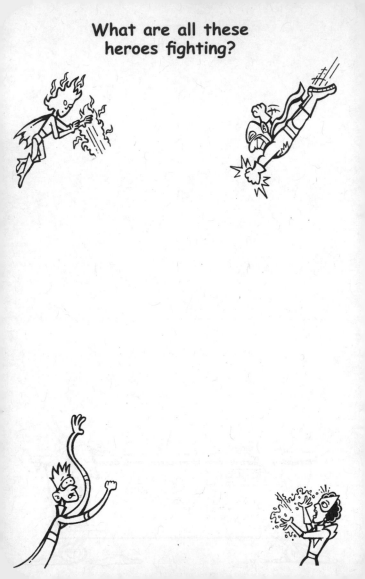

Fill the dumpster with supervillains.